Technology Takes on Nature

ICEBREAKERS

BY NICK VERONICA

Gareth Stevens
PUBLISHING

Please visit our website, www.garethstevens.com. For a free color catalog of all our high-quality books, call toll free 1-800-542-2595 or fax 1-877-542-2596.

Cataloging-in-Publication Data

Names: Veronica, Nick.
Title: Icebreakers / Nick Veronica.
Description: New York : Gareth Stevens, 2017. | Series: Technology takes on nature | Includes index.
Identifiers: ISBN 9781482457797 (pbk.) | ISBN 9781482457810 (library bound) | ISBN 9781482457803 (6 pack)
Subjects: LCSH: Icebreakers (Ships)–Juvenile literature.
Classification: LCC VM451.V47 2017 | DDC 623.82'8–dc23

First Edition

Published in 2017 by
Gareth Stevens Publishing
111 East 14th Street, Suite 349
New York, NY 10003

Copyright © 2017 Gareth Stevens Publishing

Designer: Sarah Liddell
Editor: Ryan Nagelhout

Photo credits: Cover, p. 1 Ty Milford/Getty Images; background texture used throughout Margarita Khamidulina/ Shutterstock.com; p. 5 Arria Belli/Wikimedia Commons; p. 6 Chris Jackson/Staff/Getty Images Entertainment/ Getty Images; p. 7 Per Breiehagen/Getty Images; p. 8 Ben Cranke/Getty Images; p. 9 BetacommandBot/ Wikimedia Commons; pp. 10–11 Kiselev d/Wikimedia Commons; p. 12 Islander~commonswiki/Wikimedia Commons; p. 13 Heritage Images/Contributor/Hulton Archive/Getty Images; p. 14 Tupsumato/Wikimedia Commons; p. 15 BezPRUzyn/Wikimedia Commons; p. 17 Ankara/Wikimedia Commons; p. 18 Juancat/Shutterstock.com; p. 19 Algkalv/Wikimedia Commons; p. 20 Nv8200pa/Wikimedia Commons; p. 21 Kobac/Wikimedia Commons; p. 22 Abarinov/Wikimedia Commons; p. 23 Potapov Alexander/Shutterstock.com; p. 25 Bahnfrend/ Wikimedia Commons; p. 27 (both) Hike395/Wikimedia Commons; p. 29 Hammersoft/Wikimedia Commons.

Printed in the China

CPSIA compliance information: Batch #CW17GS: For further information contact Gareth Stevens, New York, New York at 1-800-542-2595.

CONTENTS

Words in the glossary appear in **bold** type the first time they are used in the text.

BREAKING THROUGH

Throughout history, travel by water has been one of the world's most important paths for **transportation**. Humans began using boats and rafts about 50,000 years ago. Every group of people, from the Egyptians to the Vikings to modern people, has used water travel for exploration, trade, and protection.

In cold climates when the water freezes over, we need icebreakers to keep boats moving. These special boats are built to take on nature's bitter cold. Icebreakers have been in use for centuries and continue to be an important tool to help people take on the forces of nature today.

MAKING ICE

Freshwater freezes at 32°F (0°C). Salty ocean water freezes at 28.4°F (−2°C). However, a freezing air temperature doesn't mean water will instantly become ice. The water **molecules** on the surface will come in contact with the cold air first and slowly drop in temperature, gradually freezing. The longer it's cold, the thicker the ice becomes.

THE ICEBREAKER USCGC *GLACIER* APPROACHES MCMURDO STATION IN ANTARCTICA. THE LETTERS "USCGC" STAND FOR "UNITED STATES COAST GUARD CUTTER." A CUTTER IS A KIND OF SHIP.

USING THE BREAKER

Some icebreakers double as boats for scientific research, or study, but most of the time, they're just used to break ice. This helps keep trade routes open, allows people to reach and explore removed areas, maintains routes to natural resources, and even helps boats that get stuck in ice!

Nations doing research near the North and South Poles often work to improve icebreaking **technology**. The United States and Russia, for example, have been the leaders in building icebreakers, while Sweden, Finland, Canada, Denmark, and Estonia have also built or purchased multiple icebreaking boats. China, Germany, Australia, and Norway are in the process of adding to their fleets, or collection of boats.

ICEBREAKER *ODEN* IN NORWAY

WATER UNDERNEATH

When cold air covers a body of water, the water directly in contact with the air freezes before the rest. So just because the top of a lake, river, or ocean freezes doesn't mean the water below freezes! Icebreakers break up the top level of ice and open up water for boats to travel on.

7

HOW ICEBREAKERS WORK

Many people have seen icebreakers, but few know how they work. Some people think they just crash into ice hard enough to break it apart. Others think they use a pointed bow, or front of the ship, to cut through ice like a knife.

Icebreakers, however, use the shape of their bow and the ship's weight to bend ice and break it apart. While ice is very hard, it isn't flexible, or able to bend without breaking. The shape of the icebreaker's underside directs ice to the sides as the boat moves through the water.

ICEBREAKER BOW

10

U. S. COAST GUARD

USING THEIR WEIGHT

Icebreakers are built to use the pressure they put on ice to break it up, then push it aside using their thick body, called a hull. This opens up a path behind the ship for others to follow. Icebreakers only "back and ram" ice—backing up and slamming directly into an ice sheet—if they have no other choice.

MAKING A BREAKER

Not just any large boat can break up thick sea ice. Some ships are strengthened in case they run into light ice, but polar icebreakers are **designed** with cutting ice in mind. They're often graded by how many feet of ice they can break through at a given speed.

The big difference between icebreakers and other large boats is the design of the bow and hull. Icebreaker bows are angled to allow the boat to rise up on ice and crush it. Their hulls are **reinforced** to handle the force of ice pushing on the ship.

50 LET POBEDY

In 2007, Russia set afloat the largest, most powerful icebreaker in the world. Measuring more than 500 feet (152 m) long, it can break ice more than 9 feet (2.7 m) thick! Its name, *50 Let Pobedy* means "50 years of victory" and honors over 50 years since the Nazi surrender in World War II.

50 LET POBEDY

11

EARLY ICEBREAKERS

The invention of steam power helped move the first true icebreakers. One of the earliest ships was Philadelphia's *City Ice Boat No. 1.* It was built in 1837 to cut through ice in the Delaware River. The Russian tugboat *Pilot* was made into an icebreaker in 1864 and became one of the world's first to have an angled bow to help it rise on top of ice to break it.

In 1898, Russia made the *Yermak,* one of the first modern icebreakers. *Yermak* was known for its ability to break through pack ice—a large mass of ice at sea that can be several feet thick.

CITY ICE BOAT NO. 1

YERMAK

Yermak was the first icebreaker built to handle thick ice in the Baltic Sea. Built in 1898, the 320-foot (97.5 m) icebreaker was one of the world's first modern designs. *Yermak* saw action in both World War I and World War II. It was used by Russia until 1963!

13

Diesel power was the next major breakthrough in icebreaker technology. The Swedish icebreaker *Ymer* swapped steam power for a diesel-electric engine in 1933. Finland followed soon after with *Sisu*. Both ships were so successful that they were used well into the 1970s. They were both replaced by newer ships that took on their names!

Diesel-electric engines are still used in the United States' largest polar icebreaker—USCGC *Polar Star*. This modern ship, however, has newer technology such as gas-powered **turbines** that can provide an extra bit of power if needed.

POLAR SEA AT REST

The Coast Guard has been without the services of *Polar Sea*, one of its two heavy icebreakers, since an engine failure in 2010. The Coast Guard first was going to scrap, or take apart, the ship, but later decided to see if new technology could be used to put it back in the water.

SISU

RANK AND SIZE

Modern icebreakers come in many shapes and sizes. They have different levels of power and icebreaking ability depending on how large they are, when they were made, and where they will be used.

The United States Coast Guard ranks its polar cutters as heavy icebreakers, medium icebreakers, or light icebreakers, while others may be just "ice-strengthened," or reinforced, ships. Heavy icebreakers need to be able to break ice 6 feet (1.8 m) thick at a speed of 3 **knots** as well as have the ability to "back and ram" through at least 20 feet (6 m) of ice. They also generally have at least 45,000 **horsepower**.

THE *POLAR STAR*

Polar Star is the United States' only active heavy icebreaker. First commissioned, or put into use, in 1976, the ship is 399 feet (122 m) long. It can continuously cut 6 feet (1.8 m) of ice at 3 knots and can back and ram through ice 21 feet (6.4 m) thick.

HOW ICEBREAKERS NAVIGATE

Icebreakers rarely take a straight path to where they're going. Instead, they search for the path of least resistance, or the easiest way to get through ice. This means they follow leads, or openings, whenever possible.

Before going through ice **floes**, captains measure ice thickness and coverage by using both **radar** and their own sight to decide the best course. Pack ice may be harder to **navigate** through, and **pressure ridges** are very dangerous. Icebergs are avoided at all costs. If an icebreaker gets stuck, it may attempt to back and ram, reversing and running into the ice with additional power, or it may look for a different route.

ICEBERG

WHY NOT CHARGE THROUGH?

Simply going around ice may be easier than going through it, even if it takes longer. But if an icebreaker can break ice, why not just go straight through? Remember, an icebreaker is an answer to a problem. Going through ice still carries some risk. If the problem can be safely avoided by going around, there's no need to cut ice.

BREAKING LAKE ICE

While polar icebreakers receive attention for their power, size, and cost, there's also a high need for nonpolar icebreakers in the United States, Canada, and around the world. In North America, these cutters help keep open waterways such as the Great Lakes, St. Lawrence Seaway, and Hudson River, which are needed for shipping and other boating in winter.

The USCGC *Mackinaw*, based in northern Michigan, is one of the main cutters used on the Great Lakes. *Mackinaw* is 290 feet (88 m) long and has the power to break nearly 3 feet (0.9 m) of ice at 3 knots.

MACKINAW IS SMALLER THAN MOST POLAR ICEBREAKERS, BUT IS STRONG ENOUGH TO BREAK THE THINNER ICE THAT FORMS ON THE GREAT LAKES.

USCGC *HEALY*

USCGC *HEALY*

Healy is considered a medium icebreaker, but at 420 feet (128 m), it's the longest icebreaker in the United States' fleet. It's also known as a scientific research ship, having more than 4,000 square feet (371.6 sq m) of laboratory space. It can hold 50 scientists in addition to its crew.

GOING NUCLEAR

One technology American icebreakers haven't used is nuclear power. A nuclear power system costs a lot of money to build and keep running. Nuclear power also brings the possibility of a meltdown—an accident that happens when a nuclear core gets too hot. A meltdown would be deadly to people on board and the area around a ship.

Russia is the only country that has nuclear-powered icebreakers. Russia's first nuclear icebreaker was commissioned in 1957—NS *Lenin*. In 1977, its second nuclear icebreaker, NS *Arktika*, became the first ship to reach the North Pole. Today, NS *50 Let Pobedy* is Russia's most powerful nuclear-powered icebreaker.

ARKTIKA

WORLD'S BIGGEST ICEBREAKING FLEETS

RUSSIA
41 ICEBREAKERS
5 UNDER CONSTRUCTION
6 PLANNED

FINLAND
7 ICEBREAKERS
1 PLANNED

CANADA
6 ICEBREAKERS
1 PLANNED

SWEDEN
6 ICEBREAKERS

UNITED STATES
5 ICEBREAKERS
1 PLANNED

OTHER NUCLEAR SHIPS

While the United States doesn't have any nuclear icebreakers, it does have other nuclear ships and submarines. Nuclear power allows vessels to remain at sea for longer periods of time without having to refuel. The United States put the first nuclear-powered submarine into the water in 1955. Today, there are more than 140 nuclear-powered ships in the world.

GETTING STUCK

Even icebreakers can get stuck in thick polar ice. In 2013, the Chinese icebreaker *Xue Long* got stuck 6 nautical miles (11.1 km) away from a Russian ship trapped in Antarctic ice that it was trying to help. The Russian ship—MV *Akademik Shokalskiy*—had sent out a message asking for help on Christmas Day. Two other icebreakers were also on their way to help.

In early January, *Xue Long* freed itself by making a 100-degree turn in the water, breaking enough ice to make a channel in the water. A helicopter on board the icebreaker had already flown to *Akademik Shokalskiy* to move 52 scientists and tourists off the ship and to safety.

ARCTIC SCIENCE

Countries who want to explore and do research in Arctic waters need icebreakers to help their scientists reach many areas they want to study. Five countries have claims to territory in the Arctic: the United States, Russia, Canada, Norway, and Denmark. Other nations such as China have built icebreakers in recent years to study in Arctic waters as well.

CLIMATE CHANGE

You might think icebreakers may become less important to countries because of **climate change**. In fact, the opposite may be true! Less ice will likely increase the amount of shipping, tourism, and commercial activity through Arctic waters. That, in turn, has created a bigger need for governments to protect ships traveling through those areas. And as ice sheets get smaller, Arctic waters may see more ice floes ships will have to avoid.

In addition, less ice coverage is likely to increase interest in studying and exploring Antarctica and the North Pole because it is easier to boat to new areas.

SHRINKING ICE

As Earth's average temperature has risen over the last century—especially since the 1980s—ice coverage in the Northern Hemisphere has fallen sharply. This applies to areas with both seasonal and year-round ice coverage. Even places such as Glacier National Park in Montana have seen much smaller ice coverage in recent years.

GRINNELL GLACIER IN MONTANA'S GLACIER NATIONAL PARK HAS DECREASED IN SIZE SIGNIFICANTLY OVER THE LAST FEW YEARS, IN PART DUE TO CLIMATE CHANGE.

GRINNELL GLACIER, 1938

GRINNELL GLACIER, 2009

BREAKING IN THE FUTURE

As icebreaker use is likely to rise in the future, many nations are looking to add more icebreakers to their fleets. The United States only has one heavy icebreaker, while Russia has more than 40 ships ready to cut polar ice.

"The highways of the Arctic are paved by icebreakers," Alaska senator Dan Sullivan said in 2015. "Right now, the Russians have superhighways, and we have dirt roads with potholes." Many hope the US government decides to build more icebreakers, which can cost nearly $1 billion each and take many years to build. Even with climate change affecting our waters, icebreakers will continue to be an important tool for transportation in the future.

DRILLING FOR OIL

As Arctic interest grows, drilling for polar oil is likely to bring more ships into Arctic waters. The Royal Dutch Shell company, for example, has already tested drilling off the shores of northern Alaska. Many worry about bringing industry to these areas because of potential harm to the environment, but as oil companies attract more interest in this region, more icebreakers will be needed to keep these ships safe.

USCGC *HEALY*

GLOSSARY

climate change: the gradual change in Earth's weather patterns caused in part by human activity

design: to create the pattern or shape of something

floe: a sheet or mass of floating ice

horsepower: the measure of power produced by an engine

knot: one nautical mile per hour, equal to about 1.15 miles (1.85 km) per hour

molecule: the smallest bit of a substance having all the features of that substance

navigate: to find one's way

pressure ridge: a collection of ice floes stacked over time to create a large cluster of ice blocks several feet high and wide

propeller: a paddle-like part on a ship that spins in the water to move the ship forward

radar: a machine that uses radio waves to locate and identify objects

reinforce: to make stronger

technology: the way people do something using tools and the tools they use

transportation: the movement of people and things from one place to another

turbine: a series of blades moved by water used to create energy for an engine

FOR MORE INFORMATION

BOOKS

Meinking, Mary. *Who Counts the Penguins? Working in Antarctica.* Chicago, IL: Raintree, 2011.

Meister, Cari. *Icebreakers.* Minneapolis, MN: Jump!, 2017.

WEBSITES

How Icebreakers Break Ice
athropolis.com/arctic-facts/fact-icebreaker-break.htm
Learn more about how icebreakers crack ice on this site.

Icebreakers and Ice Strengthened Ships
coolantarctica.com/Antarctica%20fact%20file/History/ships/icebreaker.php
Visit this site to find out more about the ships that travel through the icy waters of Antarctica.

Publisher's note to educators and parents: Our editors have carefully reviewed these websites to ensure that they are suitable for students. Many websites change frequently, however, and we cannot guarantee that a site's future contents will continue to meet our high standards of quality and educational value. Be advised that students should be closely supervised whenever they access the Internet.

INDEX